Timeline of the Crusades

The Crusades were a series of military campaigns, backed by the church, that aimed to conquer the Holy Land from its Muslim rulers and place it under Christian control.

1096–1099
First Crusade

Pope Urban II calls for Christian knights to capture Jerusalem. The city is captured and its inhabitants are massacred.

1187–1192
Third Crusade

Jerusalem is recaptured by Muslim hero Saladin. Richard the Lionheart of England, Philip II of France, and Holy Roman Emperor Frederick I try unsuccessfully to get it back.

1144–1155
Second Crusade

Led by Holy Roman Emperor Conrad III and King Louis VII of France, the Second Crusade fails to capture Damascus.

1202–1204
Fourth Crusade

Led by Boniface of Montferrat, the expedition becomes sidetracked and attacks the Christian city of Constantinople (now Istanbul).

1212
The Children's Crusade

Led by Nicholas of Cologne and Stephen of Cloyes, many thousands of French and German children die trying to reach Jerusalem.

1270
Eighth Crusade

Louis IX dies in Tunis, never reaching Jerusalem.

1228–1229
Sixth Crusade

Holy Roman Emperor Frederick II recaptures Jerusalem.

1248–1254
Seventh Crusade

King Louis IX of France is defeated and held for ransom by an Egyptian army.

1217–1221
Fifth Crusade

Led by King Andrew II of Hungary and Duke Leopold VI of Austria, the crusade fizzles out after a heavy defeat in Egypt.

1271–1272
Ninth Crusade

The last major crusade ends in a truce between Prince Edward (later Edward I of England) and Sultan Baybars of Egypt.

Map of the Crusades

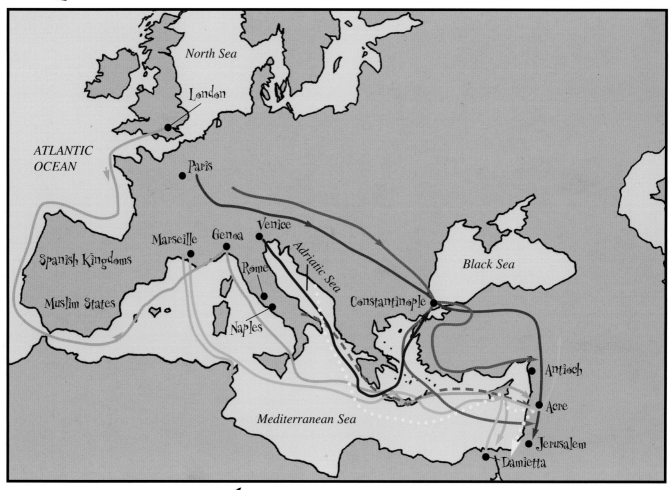

North Sea

London

ATLANTIC
OCEAN

Paris

Spanish Kingdoms

Muslim States

Marseille

Genoa

Rome

Venice

Adriatic Sea

Naples

Black Sea

Constantinople

Mediterranean Sea

Antioch

Acre

Jerusalem

Damietta

Key to the Crusades

First Crusade (1096–1099)
Second Crusade (1144–1155)
Third Crusade (1187–1192)
Fourth Crusade (1202–1204)
Fifth Crusade (1217–1221)
Sixth Crusade (1228–1229)
Seventh Crusade (1248–1254)
Eighth Crusade (1270)
Ninth Crusade (1271–1272)

Author:
Fiona Macdonald studied history at
Cambridge University and at the University of
East Anglia. She has taught adult education, and in
schools and colleges, and is the author of
numerous books for children on historical topics.

Artist:
David Antram was born in Brighton, England,
in 1958. He studied at Eastbourne College of Art
and then worked in advertising for 15 years before
becoming a full-time artist. He has illustrated
many children's nonfiction books.

Series Creator:
David Salariya was born in Dundee,
Scotland. He has illustrated a wide range of books
and has created and designed many new series for
publishers both in the UK and overseas. In 1989,
he established The Salariya Book Company. He
lives in Brighton with his wife, illustrator Shirley
Willis, and their son, Jonathan.

Editor:
Karen Barker Smith

Published in Great Britain in 2014 by
The Salariya Book Company Ltd
25 Marlborough Place, Brighton BN1 1UB

ISBN-13: 978-0-531-27100-1 (lib. bdg.)   978-0-531-23851-6 (pbk.)

All rights reserved.
Published in 2014 in the United States
by Franklin Watts
An imprint of Scholastic Inc.
Published simultaneously in Canada.

A CIP catalog record for this book is available
from the Library of Congress.

Printed and bound in China.
Printed on paper from sustainable sources.
1 2 3 4 5 6 7 8 9 10 R 24 23 22 21 20 19 18 17 16 15 14

PAPER FROM
SUSTAINABLE
FORESTS

You Wouldn't Want to Be a Medieval Knight!

How am I supposed to fight wearing this?

Armor You'd Rather Not Wear

Written by
Fiona Macdonald

Illustrated by
David Antram

Created and designed by
David Salariya

Franklin Watts®
An Imprint of Scholastic Inc.
NEW YORK • TORONTO • LONDON • AUCKLAND • SYDNEY
MEXICO CITY • NEW DELHI • HONG KONG

Contents

Introduction

You are a young boy living in England toward the end of the medieval period, around the year A.D. 1400. Your home is in a huge, splendid castle, where your father works. He helps manage its vast estates and spends most of his days in his chamber, studying old documents or checking accounts. Now that you're eight years old, your father wants you to start learning to be a castle official like him. He thinks you should be pleased at the prospect of having such a steady career. But you are horrified—that is not what you want to do!

You have always dreamed of becoming a soldier, like the knight who owns the castle. He is a famous fighting man and is one of the king's trusted champions. You admire the knight's strength, skill, and brave deeds in battle. You envy his riches, his shining armor, and his wonderful warhorse. He is your hero and you want to follow his example. But how much do you really know about his life? Are you sure you want to be a medieval knight?

Glamorous Knights

To Be a Knight

KNIGHTS are meant to follow rules of good behavior, called "chivalry." They must promise to be:

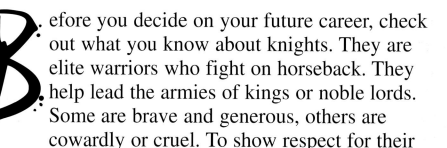

Before you decide on your future career, check out what you know about knights. They are elite warriors who fight on horseback. They help lead the armies of kings or noble lords. Some are brave and generous, others are cowardly or cruel. To show respect for their high rank, knights are always called "Sir." There have been knights for hundreds of years. They first became important around A.D. 800.

Gentle

Brave

Generous

Merciful

Oh, isn't he handsome!

Hands off, he's mine!

Pious

...and also courteous, gallant, obedient, patient, and persevering!

At that time, kings and lords recruited expert warriors to help them conquer new lands. They called such men "knights." Now, in the 15th century, these knights are sometimes replaced by professional soldiers, called "mercenaries." They will fight for anyone who will pay them.

Handy Hint

If you'd prefer a quiet life, you can pay the king a tax called "scutage," or shield money, to avoid becoming a knight.

Do You Have a Rich, Noble Family?

Not everyone can become a knight. You normally need the right family background—it helps if your father and grandfather were knights before you. Men from ordinary families can also be made knights as a reward for bravery in battle. Women cannot become knights, though they often help defend castles from attackers or accompany armies as cooks and nurses. Most knights' families own large estates, given to them long ago by the kings or lords they promised to fight for. In return for this land, knights have many duties, in peacetime as well as in war.

National Duties

FIGHTING. You'll have to fight in the king's army and lead your own troop of soldiers in war.

FRIENDSHIP. You'll have to be a good companion to the king, and share in all his hobbies.

COUNSELING. You'll have to offer the king advice—even if he doesn't like what you have to say.

Handy Hint

Your family will choose a wife to help and support you—whether you like her or not!

Local Duties

FARMING. You'll have to manage your family's land and give orders to the peasants working there.

FINANCE. You'll have to collect royal taxes. That will make you very unpopular with everyone!

LEGAL GUARDIAN. You'll have to protect the local peasants at times of conflict and also settle fights among them.

Time to Start Training

Are you ready to leave your home and family? It takes many years of training to become a knight. Most boys start at the age of eight. Your parents will send you to a well-respected knight's castle. He'll teach you many new skills, but he won't understand how homesick you'll feel. You will meet several other boys at his castle, all hoping to be knights, like you. The youngest will work as pages, or household servants, and grooms, or stable-hands. The oldest will serve as squires, or personal assistants, taking important messages, carrying weapons, leading horses, and helping knights get ready for battle.

Learning to Be a Knight

WAITING AT TABLES and serving food will teach you good manners.

BUILD UP YOUR MUSCLES. Training with heavy wooden swords will make you strong enough to fight with real weapons.

LEARNING TO HUNT with hawks will teach you to observe your surroundings and be a good lookout.

HORSE SENSE. Feeding and grooming large warhorses will teach you how to handle them when it's time to ride off to battle.

C'mon lad. If you want to be a knight you have to leave home.

TARGET PRACTICE. Riding at a quintain (a target fixed to a swiveling pole with a weight at the other end) will teach you how to fight with a lance (below).

Handy Hint

Watch out for bullies! You'll find several bigger boys training at the same castle as you.

Quintain

Ooof!

Loyalty to Your Lord

nights are meant to be loyal. They swear oaths, or solemn promises, to be faithful to the king and to their lord. The first and most important of these oaths takes place when a squire has completed his training and is ready to become a knight. This usually happens around the age of 21. The evening before the ceremony, he takes a bath and puts on clean clothes. Then he goes to the castle chapel and spends the night in prayer. The next morning, he kneels before the king—or his lord—and promises to serve him loyally. The king then dubs (taps) him on the shoulder, saying "Arise, Sir knight."

Arise, Sir knight.

THE RIGHT ROBES? The king or your lord will give you a uniform, called "livery," made to his own design. Your squire will help you dress (left).

PICTURE PUZZLE. You will have to learn how to read heraldic designs (right). Each noble family has its own coat of arms, which they'll expect you to recognize.

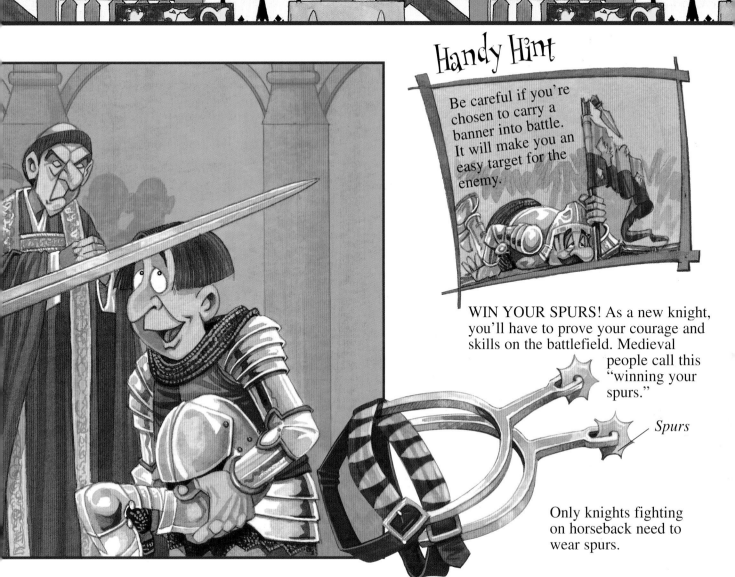

Be careful if you're chosen to carry a banner into battle. It will make you an easy target for the enemy.

WIN YOUR SPURS! As a new knight, you'll have to prove your courage and skills on the battlefield. Medieval people call this "winning your spurs."

Spurs

Only knights fighting on horseback need to wear spurs.

DON'T CHOOSE A LOSER! You'll meet many rival lords (left). Only one can bring you success. Those lords on the wrong "side"—and the knights serving them—might end up losing their lives!

WANT TO BE PAID TO FIGHT? Then join a band of mercenary soldiers (right). They'll fight for anyone who gives them money.

13

Life in a Castle

Castle Conditions

Living in a castle is not always easy, pleasant, or comfortable. How could you cope with:

You have spent all your life in other knights' castles. Do you really want one as your own home? Castles are very expensive to build, and it is dangerously hard work if you want to capture someone else's! Once you have a castle, you must keep it well repaired and pay for soldiers to guard it night and day. Inside, castles are becoming more cozy than they have been for centuries. You'll find private rooms for you and your family, with fireplaces in most rooms, and tapestries hanging on the walls. Most castles are still cold and drafty in the winter and horribly smelly in the summertime—especially when sewage from the garderobes, or toilets, leaks into the castle moat!

freezing-cold battlements;

rowdy soldiers in their quarters;

a flaming hot kitchen;

a drawbridge rising unexpectedly;

a noisy, fiery forge;

a fast-falling portcullis;

and a dismal dungeon?

Get Geared Up

ompared to ordinary foot soldiers, knights are very fortunate. They have armor to protect them in battle. In the past, this was made of chain mail but it's now usually made of "plates", or shaped pieces of metal carefully joined together. This new armor looks very impressive, but it is extremely expensive. As a new knight, you'll probably have to make do with hand-me-downs from your family.

DRESSED TO KILL. You will need help from a squire to put on your armor, but it only takes about 15 minutes. Be careful to fasten all the separate pieces properly, otherwise the result could be disastrous! First of all, put on a padded tunic which includes chain mail sections (1). Attach a chain mail kilt (2). Put on the plate armor, carefully fastening all the straps (3). Finally, add your helmet and gauntlets (4).

1

2

3

4

Visor to cover face

Breastplate

Chain mail kilt

Gauntlets (gloves)

Greaves (shin guards)

You could buy secondhand armor, or loot some from a dead knight during battle! Whether it's old or new, all armor clanks, creaks, and chafes. It's hot and heavy to wear and can slow you down, trip you, or get in the way of your weapons. Remember—even the best armor is not guaranteed to save you. In battle, you'll always have to fight for your life!

Handy Hint

Don't be old-fashioned! Remember, styles of armor change over the years.

Rivet

Metal ring

MAKING A CHAIN MAIL tunic is extremely time-consuming (above). Thousands of separate rings have to be shaped from metal wire, linked with the next one, then held in place by rivets. More modern plate armor is a little faster to create.

17

Armed and Dangerous

In battle, you will rely on your weapons. You should own five or six different kinds: a mace, a long sword, a short sword, a battle-axe, a lance, and maybe a dagger. All are sharp, awkward and heavy. Just one sword will weigh over two pounds. You must be able to handle them well, without injuring yourself. You will have to decide which weapons to use for defending yourself and which for attacking your enemies. Whichever one you choose, act quickly or an enemy soldier will kill you while you're still making up your mind! The latest lethal weapon is a war hammer. It's designed to kill knights wearing plate armor by delivering deadly blows. However, you have to be brave enough to get close to your enemy to hit him!

MACES, or clubs, have heavy metal heads on wooden and metal poles.

LONG SWORDS have sharp, double-edged blades and large handles for a good grip. Use them to slash at enemy foot soldiers.

SHORT SWORDS have small blades with sharp tips. Use them to stab enemy knights through chinks in their armor.

BATTLE-AXES have wedge-shaped blades and short wooden handles. Use them for slicing through foot soldiers' long pikes and leather garments.

18

Phew—that was close!

Coping on Crusade

Since 1096, European knights and soldiers, known as "Crusaders," have been fighting in the Holy Land—the area around the city of Jerusalem. Crusaders hope to win this land from the Muslims who have ruled it since A.D. 637. More recently, there have been Crusades in Northeastern Europe to force pagan people living there to become Christians. Most Crusaders do not return from the Holy Land but die, either on the journey or from sickness, or are killed by Muslim soldiers. These troops fight in a way that you've never seen before, shooting at the marching Crusading armies with bows and arrows before galloping away!

A Dangerous Journey...

EXPECT TO FEEL SICK as you sail to the Holy Land, especially if this is your first long journey by sea.

TRY NOT TO WORRY about being shipwrecked. Only a few of the Crusaders' ships sink on each voyage!

DON'T GET STUCK in a snowdrift as you cross the mountains. Dig yourself out quickly, or you'll die of cold!

The Holy Land is hot! Copy Muslim soldiers and wear a loose surcoat over your armor. It will help you keep cool!

to a Dangerous Place

KEEP FLEAS OUT of your tent in the Holy Land. They carry the germs that cause plague, which can kill you!

STAY AWAY FROM SNAKES! Most are not poisonous, but their bites can be very painful.

DON'T RUN OUT OF WATER in the desert. Always carry plenty with you, or you'll die of thirst!

Surviving a Siege

Sieges are sometimes the only way to capture castles or walled cities. You need patience and huge war machines to carry out a successful siege. You must organize your army to surround the enemy city or castle, and give them orders to stop anyone from entering or leaving. Then, you have to wait until the supplies of food and water run out inside so inhabitants either starve or surrender. If you are clever or cruel you might torture enemy captives outside the walls, to warn defenders what will happen if they don't give in.

Germ Warfare

SPREAD SICKNESS by polluting enemy water supplies with the rotting corpses of dead animals. Germ-laden dead bodies can also be hurled over enemy walls.

CLEVER "CAT" (movable shed). This shelters soldiers digging tunnels under enemy walls to make them crumble and collapse.

22

Handy Hint

If you want to survive a siege, surrender right away. If the besiegers manage to break in, you won't live long.

TREBUCHET. When one end is pulled down, the other shoots up and flings rocks high over enemy defenses.

Keep up the bombardment men! Their defenses won't hold much longer.

BRUTAL BATTERING RAM. Made of a huge tree trunk tipped with iron, a battering ram is strong enough to smash holes in gates and crack stonework.

BIG BELFRY—that's what the soldiers call this tall siege tower. From the top, they can shoot arrows at defenders on the battlements.

MURDEROUS MANGONEL. This huge catapult can hurl huge lumps of rock through the air. Its power comes from ropes twisted tightly, then released.

Bravery in Battle

Look Out For:

GUNNERS, who try to kill you with shot (stone or metal balls); longbowmen, who try to kill you with sharp, feathered, arrows; and crossbowmen, who try to kill you with metal bolts.

Gun (used from c. 1400)

Longbow

Crossbow

n battle, you'll face many different types of fighters, as well as other knights. Most enemy troops will be foot soldiers. They make up the majority of most medieval armies and are recruited from rough, tough peasants. Many of these soldiers are angry at being ordered away from their fields by their king or lord. They

want to win battles quickly and then go home, which can make them vicious enemies! Compared with knights, most foot soldiers are only part-time fighters, but this does not make them any less dangerous. They are armed with various types of deadly weapons, including pikes, pitchforks, and wooden clubs. Their bows shoot bolts and arrows that fall like "killer rain" on the enemy, including you!

Handy Hint

Bind up wounds with egg-soaked bandages and stop bleeding by cauterizing wounds with a red-hot iron.

Don't Fall Off Your Horse!

A knight's most important possessions are his warhorses. Fierce stallions, called "destriers" and "coursers," are specially bred for battle. Warhorses must be extremely strong to carry knights plus their weapons and armor. By nature they are aggressive and are also trained to bite and kick. A good warhorse is very expensive and you'll need at least two! Knights also need packhorses to carry baggage, and riding horses for squires and grooms.

IN BATTLE, you line up alongside other knights, holding your lance "couched," or braced against your side. When you dig your spurs into his side, your horse will charge toward the enemy!

Beware!

STAY AWAY FROM STAKES! Half buried, pointing upward, these sharp wooden poles kill many horses and riders.

CHAAARGE!

BEWARE OF BOGS! Don't let damp, soggy ground trap you and your horse and sink your chance of victory.

PREPARE FOR PITS! Your enemies will dig pits, then cover them with leaves or grass so you will fall into them.

Caltrops

BE CAREFUL OF CALTROPS! These iron spikes are scattered on the ground and cruelly dig into horses' hooves.

26

So Many Ways to Die...

From the start of your training as a knight, your life will be at risk. It's hard to know for sure, but most fighting men die before they are 50 years old. All knights hope to be remembered after they die. Many pay artists to create lifelike portraits of them to be displayed in the church where they will be buried. They pay priests to say prayers and give money to charity so that poor people will remember them gratefully. If you plan on becoming a knight, do as others do and order your tomb right away!

Try Not to...

DIE IN BATTLE, in pain, and surrounded by the enemy.

DIE FROM INFECTED WOUNDS, a miserable, lingering death.

DIE FROM DYSENTERY, an awful sickness.

DIE IN PRISON, locked in chains, then abandoned.

DIE FROM HEATSTROKE, half cooked inside your armor.

DIE FROM FROSTBITE, shivering and chilled to the bone.

BE SEVERELY INJURED and unable to work for the rest of your life.

And Try to...

DIE PEACEFULLY IN YOUR BED. That is actually how many retired knights end their days!

Glossary

Banner A flag carried by a knight who commanded other knights.

Bolt A short arrow, fired by a crossbow.

Caltrops Sharp metal spikes that are scattered in front of horses to wound them and stop them from advancing.

Cauterize To burn body tissue in order to seal it and stop bleeding.

Chivalry Rules of good behavior that all knights were meant to follow.

Coat of arms Badge worn by a knight to show he belonged to a noble family.

Courteous Polite and considerate.

Crusades Wars fought between Christians and Muslims for the right to rule the Holy Land.

Dub To tap on the shoulder with a sword. It is part of the ceremony of becoming a knight.

Dysentery An infectious disease that causes terrible sickness and diarrhea.

Elite Best, or highest-ranking.

Gallant Brave, unselfish, and romantic.

Garderobes Toilets. The word means "guard clothes"—medieval people believed that the smell from bathrooms kept away insects that ate woollen cloth.

Heraldic Belonging to heraldry—the study of coats of arms.

Livery Uniform worn by soldiers fighting in the same knight's army.

Medieval Belonging to the Middle Ages (the years from around A.D. 1000 to A.D. 1500).

Mercenary soldiers (or **mercenaries**) Soldiers who fought for anyone who would pay them.

Page A young boy who worked as a servant in a noble family's household.

Persevering Refusing to give in when faced with danger or difficulty.

Pike An axe-shaped metal blade plus a sharp metal spike fitted to the end of a long pole.

Pious Deeply religious and devoted to the Christian Church.

Pitchfork A huge, two-pronged fork on the end of a long pole, usually used as a farming tool.

Plague A deadly disease, also known as the Black Death, caused by bacteria (germs) that were passed from rats to humans by fleabites.

Plate armor Armor made from pieces of metal, carefully shaped and fitted together.

Portcullis A metal gate that dropped down to bar the entrance to a castle.

Quintain Device used for practice fighting. It was made of a swiveling wooden pole with a target at one end and a heavy weight at the other.

Scutage Tax paid by men from rich or noble families who did not want to become knights.

Spurs Sharp spikes, fixed to the heel-pieces of a knight's footwear. They were pressed into a horse's side to make it run more quickly.

Squire A young man who worked as personal assistant to a knight.

Surcoat Long, loose robe worn on top of armor, often decorated with a knight's coat of arms.

Tournaments Mock battles fought by knights for fun and as training for war.

Index

What Is Chivalry?

There was more to being a knight than just fighting and hunting—there was also chivalry. The word comes from an old French word for "horseman," but it came to mean a code of conduct that knights were supposed to follow. Books of chivalry advised knights to protect the weak, defend the church, and fight for women.

The earliest knights were rough fighting men. Their exploits were celebrated in epic poems—exciting tales of valor in which women are rarely mentioned.

During the twelfth century, attitudes began to change. The idea arose that knights should be perfect gentlemen, being fair and merciful to their enemies and behaving in a gracious manner to ladies. Long poems called *romances* became fashionable, in which knights perform valiant deeds for the love of a lady. (The most famous stories of this kind are the tales of King Arthur and his Round Table.) Poets known as *troubadours* began to compose extremely polite love songs addressed to noble ladies at the courts.

The church did not approve of love songs, but it did want to improve the behavior of fighting men. It tried to limit bloodshed by banning fighting on certain days, and it opposed the tournament violence and deaths.

Top Medieval Ladies

French heroine **Joan of Arc (1412–1431)** believed she heard the voices of angels telling her to fight for the Dauphin, the heir to the French throne. She drove the English from the city of Orléans, allowing the Dauphin to be crowned as King Charles VII. She was captured and sold to the English, who found her guilty of witchcraft and heresy. She was only 19 when she was burned at the stake in 1431. In 1920, she was named a saint.

Charles gave Joan a holy banner (a sign of leadership) decorated with a picture of Jesus Christ and two angels.

Greek historian **Anna Comnena (1083–1153)** was the daughter of the emperor of Byzantium. She wrote *The Alexiad*, an account of her father's reign.

Eleanor of Aquitaine (1122–1204) was married to King Henry II of England. Two of her ten children also became kings of England: Richard I and John. She led them both in rebellion against their father. She was also a patron of music and the arts.

Did You Know?

• It was bad form to kill a knight after he had been defeated in battle. Instead, captured knights were ransomed—allowed to go after their followers had paid money for their release.

• In England and Wales, the High Court of Chivalry judged disputes between knights, including disagreements about who had the right to wear a particular coat of arms. The court still exists, but rarely meets.

What Happened to the Knights?

By the early sixteenth century, knights were losing their importance. More and more countries had professional armies, and the knight with his lance was no match for their ranks of soldiers with pikes. Nor did the knight's armor protect him against guns. Armorers tried making thicker breastplates that were somewhat like a bulletproof vest. Sometimes a second breastplate was strapped over the first one. Not surprisingly, knights often refused to wear such heavy armor. Sometimes they would leave off their heavy leg pieces and wear boots instead. By the mid-seventeenth century, the armored horseman was on his way out.

The knight's home, the castle, also fell out of fashion. This was partly because knights demanded more comfortable housing. But it was also because of the increasing use of cannons. At first, openings for cannons were made in the existing castle walls. Then, starting in France and Italy, cannons were set on low, thick, earth-filled bastions instead. These became the artillery forts of the sixteenth century, which were no longer a knight's private home but a government garrison.

Harquebusiers

These mid-seventeenth-century horsemen wore tough, buff leather coats, breastplates, and elbow gauntlets on their left arms. Their helmets had triple-barred visors to stop a sword slash. They carried pistols as well as swords. Their name comes from the word *arquebus,* which originally meant an early long-barreled matchlock gun, but later referred to a handheld gun.